LEAVE *the* 99

FOR *the* 1

Wyatt & Sons Publishers books may be ordered through booksellers or by contacting:

Wyatt & Sons Publishers, LLC
Mobile, Alabama 36695
www.wyattpublishing.com
editor@wyattpublishing.com

Because of the dynamic nature of the Internet, any web address or links contained in this book may have changed since publication and may no longer be valid.

Cover illustration: shutterstock
Cover design by: Mark Wyatt
Interior design by: Mark Wyatt

ISBN 13:978-1-954798-27-4
Printed in the United States of America

LEAVE the 99 FOR the 1

by

MARGARET ABBOTT

W/S

WYATT & SONS
PUBLISHERS, LLC
Mobile, Alabama

Dedication

I dedicate this book to those who encouraged me to write it and to the many who knew and loved Paul. Also, to all those who have lost a child no matter the age. He truly does comfort all who mourn, He gives us beauty for ashes, the oil of joy for mourning, the garment of praise for the spirit of heaviness. (*Isaiah 61:2-3, paraphrased*).

Finding Paul

Paul was born on May 23, 1969; and it was one of the happiest days of my life. After having a little boy in 1963 who was not expected to live, I was thrilled to have a healthy beautiful baby boy and I could not sleep all night. Paul was one of those kids who could do what he set out to do. When he was around 7, I remember looking out of our window and seeing this child dive in the pool as if he had always been doing it. It was Paul. When he tried skiing, it was the same way – like he had always been doing it.

Paul grew up in Ephrata, Pennsylvania. He was a Senior Patrol Leader in Boy Scouts, graduated from Ephrata High School in 1987 where he was on the diving team. He attended Pierce Jr. College and Drexel University both in Philadelphia and Arcadia University in Glenside, Pennsylvania where he played soccer.

Throughout his life, he worked as a waiter, landscaper, and fram¬ing houses which he enjoyed the most. He loved to travel and camp all over the southwest, Bend, Oregon, and San Clemente, California where he spent 17 years before moving to Venice, Florida in 2019. Paul enjoyed rock climbing, surfing, camping, and reading.

Paul had an amazing sense of humor and was loved by all who knew him. I only wish he knew how amazing he was and that everyone loved him. Unfortunately, Paul, like so many others believe lies about themselves.

Skipping ahead to the past 18 years, we had not seen Paul for 17 years and had not heard from him since 2011. He had spent many years traveling the country. We suspected that he was in California but did not know for sure. In 2018, the Holy Spirit spoke to me and said that "this kind can only come out with prayer and fasting." This "kind" in the Greek means genos – generations, family. I sensed that He wanted me to fast wine for Paul which I did. Five months later, I received a letter in the mail from a young man in California, Garrett, who had befriended Paul. Garrett sent his email address and phone number. I called him immediately and grilled him to make sure that it was not a scam. I later asked him to send me a picture of Paul so that I would know that he knew him which he did. Paul did not contact us but I was in contact with Garrett often during that year.

While in Maine in July of 2019, I was writing in my

journal and heard the Holy Spirit say to leave the 99 and go for the 1. When I googled it to find the exact scripture, the song Reckless Love came up.......... *He chases me down, fights til I'm found – leaves the 99.* When I mentioned it to Ray, he told me about a Word that came to him earlier in the year when he read the story of Joseph. Jacob said, "my son is alive, I will go to him". We both knew we were supposed to go, and it was confirmed by our last two visits to family and friends on the Cape.

We left Cape Cod at about 4:00 PM and drove as far as Wilkes-Barre, Pennsylvania the first day and enjoyed a free night at the Red Roof Inn and stopped in Columbus, Ohio the next night and spent the night with friends and were encouraged by the visit. We left the next morning with a packed lunch from our friends and stopped in Indiana to relax and eat lunch. That night, we drove as far as Effingham, Illinois. We were very tired from the ride and time change but enjoyed a good night's sleep – God is good! My Word from Holy Spirit in the morning was Zephaniah 3:17, "The Lord your God is in your midst, a warrior who saves. He will rejoice over you with joy. He will be quiet in His love making no mention of past sins. He will rejoice over you with shouts of joy"! I sensed Him saying to me that my plans would be fulfilled with perfect faithfulness.

That day, we drove through Missouri and went as far as Miami, Oklahoma staying at anice Microtel.

I was encouraged with Ezekiel 11:19, "And I will give them one heart (a new heart) and I will put a new spirit within them; and I will take the stony (unnaturally hardened) heart out of their flesh and will give them a heart of flesh (sensitive and responsive to the touch of their God). As I thought about I Peter 3:7 in the night, I realized that I had allowed myself to become anxious and not TRUST You, Father. I repented and put my trust and confidence back in Him.

I will be still and wait patiently for You. Thank You for inner peace and spiritual well-being.

Our steps were being ordered by Him. He granted us strength and made us able because He considered us faithful and trustworthy to do what He called us to do. I was reminded of the many prophecies that I had received about Paul through the years, and we were able to continue the fight of faith knowing that He would do His work which was unusual and incredible and would accomplish this extraordinary work. That day we drove across Oklahoma to Amarillo, Texas. It was a nice day. The next day, I read in Isaiah 30 that He longs to be gracious and have compassion on us. We spent a little time in Amarillo getting an oil change, haircuts, and a gun case as we were heading for California. The ride from there to Albuquerque was filled with brush ranches and mountains.

When we stopped, I made a reservation in San Clemente arriving Saturday for 6 nights. We had not heard back from Garrett at that point but kept trusting God.

O Lord, be gracious to us, we have waited expectantly for You.

Heard back from Garrett that morning. We had a beautiful ride through New Mexico and Flagstaff to Phoenix. We got a room at Baymont and were so tired that we ordered Chinese food delivered. As I started to read Psalm 40 the next morning, the first thing that I saw was the introduction: God Sustains His Servant – thank You, Father! Ray and I prayed verses 1-3 for Paul, "I waited patiently for the Lord; and He inclined to me, and heard my cry. He also brought me up out of a horrible pit, out of the miry clay, and set my feet upon a rock, and established my steps. He has put a new song in my mouth – Praise to our God; many will see it and fear, and will trust in the Lord."

The scenery from Arizona to California was very interesting. We arrived in San Clemente around 4:30 PM. We had a nice 2-room suite which I did not realize when I booked it. We contacted Garrett, and he invited us to his home church for the next morning. We met Garrett for the first time when we arrived at his house for home church. It was the closest thing that I have ever seen to I Corinthians 14. We love the way that each person had a Word, a song, etc. Several sang acapella including Garrett who sang "Living Hope." This song always touches me now whenever I hear it and think of Garrett. Holy Spirit was there ministering through each one. That group of people greatly ministered to us and prayed for us and prophesied over us at the end of the meeting.

We went out for lunch with them afterwards to Whole Foods. Garrett told us some of the places to look for Paul; and when he was not working, he drove us around. Lord, You have heard my prayer, You have seen my tears. You will love Paul's life from the pit of destruction. You will cast all his sins behind Your back.

We received a phone call from our brother-in-law saying that my 99-year-old mother was not doing well. Quite often when God is working, the enemy will try to interfere. I prayed that God would preserve His purpose for her. I had peace about it, and she ended up being fine. I had a time of intercessory prayer and worship for Paul with Living Hope and Come Out of Hiding. As I sang these lyrics: And oh, as you run, what hindered love will only become part of the story.

Monday morning, we took a drive to look at the pier and beach. We got a sandwich at Rose's and sat downtown at Del Mar and El Camino for 4 hours watching everyone who got off the buses and trolleys. We rode by the homeless encampment, got pizza at Sonny's, and ate it at the pier to see the sunset. We could not believe that there was a train rail right there at the pier and saw a train go by. We had a great conversation with a conservative Californian (rare). Lawrence was in the wine business and seriously thought about leaving California.

The next day, my Word from Holy Spirit was all about hope. For whatever was thus in former days was written for our instruction that by (our steadfast and patient) endurance and the encouragement (drawn) from the Scriptures we might hold fast to and cherish HOPE. Romans 15:4

May the God of hope fill you with all joy (and peace in believing (through the experience of your faith) that by the power of the Holy Spirit you will abound in HOPE. Romans 15:13

And there it was again in Psalm 43:5B, Hope in God and wait expectantly for Him, for I shall again praise Him.

My Facebook memory that day was II Timothy 1:7, "For God has not given us a spirit of fear but of love, power, and a sound, well-balanced mind, discipline, and self-control"! I prayed that for Paul. As we were out looking, Garrett told me that Paul liked to read about lions. I thought that was interesting because Jesus is the Lion of Judah and He encourages us to be bold as lions. Paul was a very brave person.

II Timothy 1 was so encouraging to me. Apostle Paul mentioned that Onesiphorus eagerly searched for him and found him. It encouraged me to believe that we would find our Paul.

Garrett picked us up at 10:00. We looked several places until 2:00 – even where Paul use to camp. We even went to the Sheriff's office. They notified the homeless officer with his picture. No one had seen him for a while. We laid hands on and prayed for the officer while we were there.

When we got back to our hotel, I was a little discouraged and thought, "we've been looking for 2 days and nothing"! Holy Spirit reminded me that on the 3rd day, they found Jesus in the Temple!

The next morning, we went to the Buddhist Temple, but it was closed. Paul use to identify as a Buddhist/Christian as if there is any such thing! Then we went to San Clemente State Park. The officer let us ride around the campground. We rode downtown and up Pico. That afternoon, Garrett came and took us to a lot of places and had a lot of leads but no one had seen Paul for a while. A woman at Family Services said, "I know Paul." She talked about how nice he was. She put a note in Paul's file to say that we were there if he stopped in again.

Later, we went to Dana Point where a lot of homeless people go as there are people there who offer them a lot of services. Then we had dinner at Brussels Bistro in San Clemente with Garrett.

God continued to encourage us as we read His Word each morning. We looked all week without finding him. One day, Ray and I rode the red and blue line trolleys to the end with no sign of Paul.

On Thursday, August 15, I was reading my journal from August 15, 2018 where I had recorded a dream that I had. In the dream, Ray and I and another person were visiting someone in a hospital who was bound.

I told Garrett that even though the hospital said that Paul was not there, I knew we had to check out that hospital in Laguna Beach which we did in the afternoon. Paul was not there, but someone suggested that we check the ER.

The gentlemen in ER checked the computer and told us that Paul had been there on August 5. So, if you do not journal, it is a wonderful way to look back and see the things that God speaks to you and the dreams and visions that you have; you might not have any idea what they mean then, but you will probably find out later. Plus, I do not even remember that I had them until I read my journal!

We left the ER and prayed about which way to go. I told Garrett to go left which we did. Ray saw a strip mall and said we should go there. We went into a grocery store and showed Paul's picture to a cashier. She said that he had been there in the past few weeks. When we went outside, a woman approached us and said that she overheard our conversation. She was a believer and was telling us about a situation with her daughter so we prayed for her.

She told us some about a park to look for him. He was not there, and it was getting dark so we headed back to San Clemente.

I prayed that Holy Spirit would lead us and send His angel and take us to the place we needed to go. We did not find Paul that day and were scheduled to leave the next day.

We stopped at a burger place in San Clemente. Garrett

suggested we pray about staying another day. Ray was in the restroom when he said that. When he came out, he said, "Margaret, if you want to stay another day, we can do that"!

I prayed that God would let us see His glory that day. Garrett picked us up the next morning. He had discovered a place in Laguna Beach called the Box so we went there and started showing Paul's picture. People were telling us that they think they saw him that morning. The attendants showed us where he had signed in PAUL DAVID WHITE! The van driver overheard conversations and told us that he had just dropped Paul off in front of Starbucks and that he was on crutches. We headed for downtown Laguna Beach and parked on "Legion Street." We started walking downtown. We stopped at one Starbucks but they had not seen Paul that day. We continued to walk. When we got to a small convenience store, I went inside and showed the man Paul's picture. He had not seen him that day.

While I was in there, Garrett called to me and said that he saw Paul's crutches and Paul sitting in front of the Starbucks up the street. He walked up to him, gave him a fist pump, and told Paul that he brought a couple of friends. I walked up to Paul, and he put his hand out to me like he had been doing to people since he was 5 years old and said, "hi, I'm Paul. I said, "hi, I'm Margaret.

Paul said, "my mother's name is Margaret." I said, "I'm your mother." We both hugged and cried.

Paul wanted us to stay there talking to him. We stayed there for about 2 hours sitting on the sidewalk (I was 78 then). He said, "I cannot believe that my parents are here"! He was tired of drinking and wanted to quit so we offered to take him back to Venice. We took him back to our hotel which had another room and rested for 2 more nights. During that time, Paul said to me, "Mom, I don't think I ever said the L word, I love you"! We were sitting on the bed on Saturday afternoon, and he started relaying to me the story of when Joseph and Mary lost Jesus for a few days and found him in the temple.

Interesting that after looking for a few days and not finding Paul, I was discouraged and reminded God of that story.

Paul also shared with me about reading the story of Black Hawk Down. The military men were talking over a loud speaker and saying that they were not leaving without the man they came for. So, we had a good laugh over me saying that we were not leaving without PAUL DAVID WHITE!

We decided to stay another night to relax and do laundry before we headed back to Venice, Florida. We took Paul to the Thrift Store in San Clemente and met Billy who had prayed for him earlier in the week when we went in there and JP who started The Ranch (a rehabilitation place) and this thrift store which gives people coming out of rehab a place to work. JP took our picture with Paul and was so happy that we had found him.

That night, we heard Paul talking to himself (demons). I got up and talked to him and prayed, but when I mentioned something about being set free, he got agitated so I just sat and rubbed his shoulder for comfort. Paul said it was like laying on of hands.

We left San Clement the next morning at 10 and drove as far as Phoenix. We had a good trip.

I prayed, "Father, let my mouth speak wisdom, and the meditation of my heart will be understanding! Help me to be kind and conciliatory and gentle, showing unqualified consideration and courtesy toward everyone."

I read, For the Lord will go before you, and the God of Israel will be your rear guard.

We had a nice peaceful ride from Phoenix to El Paso. We were awake mostly from 3:15 AM on as Paul was unsettled. Lord, thank You for Your inner calm and spiritual well-being. Thank You also for the way people have treated Paul with favor even some praying for him and giving him $100. I sensed that because of our prayers for him, he had received a lot of favor.

We stayed in Kerrville, Texas the next night – a place that Ray and I had visited before visiting friends who were missionaries and visiting the huge Cross on the hill and prayer garden.

The next night was also a long night with little sleep as

Paul decided to take a bath in the night and filled the tub so high that we were concerned that he would drown so we stayed awake until he was back in bed.

Lord, You, are an awesome God.

We drove to Lake Charles, Louisiana. We had to go through San Antonio and Houston in the rain and traffic slowed down, but we had a great sleep. Thank You, Jesus! Father, Your loving kindness endures all day long.

"When you walk, your steps will not be impeded for your path will be clear and open; and when you run, you will not stumble." Proverbs 4:12 This Word came to me that morning while I was still in bed and heard Paul tell Ray, "When I walk...." I shared that scripture with Paul. Ray shared Psalm 103 with him.

It was a long ride from Lake Charles to Crestview, Florida, but we had a good sleep. Thank You, Jesus! I prayed Isaiah 60:1-2 over Paul.

As we drove toward Florida that week, we had no idea what the next step was. Ray called our friend, Bill, and he suggested that we go straight to the ER at Sarasota Memorial Hospital. We arrived there at 6:15 PM and were met by our daughter, Maureen, and Bill and Norma. Paul willingly checked in. He had a heart murmur and more seriously, the start of cirrhosis of the liver. We stayed until around 1:00 AM. The doctor said that they would get him a transfer to First Step Detox.

The next morning, I prayed that He would be the sustainer of his soul for You have rescued him from every trouble. I also prayed for Paul to have good soil and a teachable heart and would be rooted deep in His love. I prayed for myself that I would keep my confidence in Him. Paul was admitted to Sarasota Memorial. They were checking his heart and would do an upper and lower GI after withdrawals.

Ray and I prayed that He would give us wisdom to know what was best for Paul, whether it was rehab or something else. I prayed for Paul for total surrender and obedience to the Lord Jesus Christ and to give him a hunger and thirst for the living God.

The next day, Paul looked better, but he was very irritable and trying to get out of bed. He was upset that we did not go right to our condo. Maureen, Sammy, and Hannah came to see him. Maureen cut his hair.

Once again, I spent time in worship to praise Jesus as I prayed for Paul. That night, I confessed my anxiety as I was concerned about finding a ministry that did deliverance. Then Holy Spirit reminded me of Luke 4:18 and Isaiah 61 and that He had called me to that. "Forgive me, Jesus! Give me the grace to trust You completely"!

I prayed for Paul, "I let Myself be sought by those who did not ask for Me. I let Myself be found by those who did not seek Me. I said, here am I. As I prayed, I had a vision of Jesus carrying Paul like a lamb! What I did not realize until after Paul's passing was that Jesus was carrying Paul like a lamb to be with Him!

Paul was doing better the next day. As we were waiting for the results of the endoscopy, nurse Jan was telling him what great potential he had. Sadly, many people saw his potential except him.

I prayed a lot of warfare prayer over Paul, and I sensed the Lord say that He did not call me to anything that He would not be right there with me, and He truly was.

Paul was discharged with a wheelchair and a walker. For some reason, the hospital did not get him into the rehab. We got a portable potty and shower chair, Ensure, and other supplies. Maureen came over for 4 or 5 hours. Sammy came and installed grip bars in the bathroom. Ray and I took turns in the night. Paul had been able to get to the bathroom. Was sleeping on and off. He got in the shower in the night but had to crawl back to bed. I thanked the Lord for giving us strength for the journey.

This word came to me in the night when I asked the Lord why Paul seems to turn his head at anything written or said about Jesus. "Shame" was His answer. Satan loves to keep people bound in fear and keeps them ignorant of God's Word that says that we can come boldly to His throne of grace to receive mercy for our failures and grace just in time when we need it!

We had a few accidents to clean up, but Paul seemed to be getting stronger. He got a Klondike bar out of the freezer. Maureen, Hannah, and some of the younger ones came over to visit. Hannah gave him a shave. We watched a movie that night. Ray and I had been taking turns sleeping. Thank You, Jesus, that we had a quiet night.

We were waiting for Home Health to come. Paul had been eating a little better. He had a rash. We thought that it was from a bracelet with oils, but we found out later that it had something to do with too much ammonia in his system. He had some French toast and orange juice but was tired and agitated.

Father with You, all things are possible! Father, what should we pray, that Paul would desire freedom and deliverance?

Besides what we were experiencing being with Paul, we experienced false accusations from another person. Father, we know that Satan is the accuser of the brethren. "Through God we will have victory, for He will trample down our enemies"! Lord, we cry out to You, and You send our Your warring angels against the enemy, and they return to their own land in shame.

Lord, we do not know what to do, but our eyes are on You. We will worship You, and the God of Peace will soon crush Satan under our feet. Romans 16:20

Paul has been drinking water and juices and eating more – even meat. He had been refusing to eat meat until our friend, Bill, came over and told him that he had to eat meat to get strong.

I spent a lot of time in worship early in the morning especially about the blood of Jesus.

We took him for a ride around Venice Island. He spent most of the afternoon in his room. He did not sleep well the night before. We had an argument. He got over it. Then he made attempts at walking. He was determined to walk as one of the doctors at Sarasota Memorial said that he would never walk again.

Later that evening, we were watching the movie Taken. Paul leaned over and fell on my lap. I thought that he was dead, but he was having a seizure.

He was released from the hospital way too soon. I called 911 and was frustrated that they kept asking me so many questions. They did assure me that the ambulance was on the way. We chose for him to go to Venice Hospital because it was a block away.

I prayed that the Father would lead Paul to the rock that is Higher, Christ Jesus! You have given him the inheritance of those who fear Your Name with reverence. He will sing praise to Your Name forever. I will have faith in You constantly. I do not doubt your unlimited power. I have confident trust that the things I have asked for him in prayer will be done.

Paul was admitted to Venice Hospital. We went over and held him down for about 45 minutes while they did an

EEG to determine the chance of another seizure and how much seizure medication to give him. He had too much ammonia in his blood probably causing the itching. We spent most of the next day at the hospital. Paul was not as medicated as he had been. He said that he slept well but was not at all sociable. In fact, he stayed under the covers most of the day.

Paul got up to go in the bathroom against the doctor's orders. John, the nurse came to help him get back in bed, and he asked for help the next time. Maureen also came to visit him that day. Nurse Lisa said that his ammonia level was down.

His MRI results looked good so he was checked out by physical therapy and released. He seemed a little calmer and worked some on a word find book. Maureen and her family including Sammy came over with barbeque chicken. Paul had already eaten.

We were up real early. Paul was making bacon and eggs. I was exhausted and needed a power snooze. Paul was awake most of the day. We had a good day, watched a movie with him, he had Physical Therapy, went to Publix with us and used the walker. Later in the day, we played dominoes. Thank you, Lord, for a good day. We also got into watching football with him.

I had a hard time going to sleep that night but finally slept well until close to 8:00. Paul says that he was up all night and was itching again. He made Ray and I a heart with playdough.

It seems like he really appreciated all we were doing for him, but the spirits that came against Jesus like envy, jealousy, resentment, scorn, mockery, ridicule came against us through Paul.

Then he was being very independent with the Medicaid information, and I was feeling very stressed so I went for a pedicure to relax. I still felt stress in my neck even though I listened to worship music. I came home and laid on my bed listening to a 6-minute message by Bill Johnson on the Word of God. Holy Spirit reminded me of Daniel 11:32b...." but those who know their God will be strong and do exploits for God"! The stress left – praise God! I then spoke to Paul about not tolerating his "independence" again until he is independent. Thank You, Jesus.

Father, let me hear Your voice clearly throughout the day and speak the Words that You put in my mouth.

I woke up the next morning to Paul's room being totally trashed with cereal, brown sugar, and white sugar strewn all over the room. Chocolate milk, regular milk, and orange juice were behind the bed. Almond milk was sitting in a drawer. Clothes, books, and papers were thrown about.

My Camden pottery crock was smashed. Everything was coated with sugar. Ray saw Paul walking naked out of the bedroom trying to wrap the plastic sheet around himself. It was a very frightening scene to say the least. I believe it was what some would call a black out or hallucinations.

Not knowing exactly what we should do, Ray called the police. They came but could not Baker Act him because he did not harm himself or anyone else. They recommended that we call First Step in Sarasota which we did, but they said that they could not help him and to call Coastal Behavioral.

They told us to take him right up there for an evaluation. His condition was obvious to them so that took him to the Sarasota Memorial Hospital ER to check out his physical condition and medications. SMH ended up admitting him, and Coastal told us that they would Baker Act Paul back to them after he was cleared by the hospital. That did not happen!

A case worker at SMH called me for information. I shared a lot of our story with her about finding him in San Clemente. She was a Christian and said, "Wow, what a testimony, and we know what the root cause is"!!!

I continued to be encouraged by God's Word and by the anointed men of God that I listened to.

We visited Paul all afternoon the next day at SMH. He was mostly grouchy toward us and real antagonistic toward the psychiatrist. He would not tell the doctor why he was there, but the only thing that he would tell the doctor is that I use to beat him all the time!!! They also had a sitter with him the whole time he was there for this visit so that he would not get out of bed on his own.

Maureen and Asiah came in to visit him, but he was grouchy with them also. She let him know that he would be dead if we had not gone to California to find him. Maureen let him know that she does not remember any beatings.

His brother Gary and wife, Terry called to see how he was doing. Gary said that it sounded like Paul was going through what he went through which was a need for deliverance. Gary did not remember any beatings either!

The next day, I was reading the Word but hearing the words to a song...." earth has no sorrow that heaven cannot heal. I was also reminded of the song Come As You Are by Crowder and Revelation 21:4, "And God shall wipe away all tears from their eyes; and there shall be no more death, neither sorrow, nor crying, neither shall there be any more pain: for the former things are passed away"! I continued to be encouraged by God's Word.

SMH had Paul on Ativan for anxiety. He was sleeping well but mentioned that he only weighed 121 so he was going to eat whether he was hungry or not. He was in a good mood when we got there and was talking about the Steelers and the Patriots, but he was irritable before we left.

The next day, the psychiatrist and Special Nurse questioned him. He would not give them straight answers and got angry when I did and would not speak to me the rest of the day. He did not speak to Ray or Maureen either. Father, our trust is in You.

I was sensing that I was to go through all my pictures that had Paul in them and make him an album. I continued to pray the Word of God over Paul.

He was in a better mood the next day although he stayed covered up a lot. Come to think of it, he worked for a time at Moody's Diner in Maine and would call it his diner because he admitted to being "moody."

SMH was getting him up walking again and said that they were working on getting him in Coastal Behavioral. Gary, the sitter, was in tears when I told him about going to San Clemente and finding Paul.

The next day, I was hearing the word "sabotage" which means deliberate destruction carried out by an enemy and earlier heard "Apollyon" which means a destroyer. John 10:10 says that the thief comes only in order to steal, kill, and destroy, but I came that they may have and enjoy life, and have it in abundance. The enemy was definitely out to destroy Paul's life!

The next day, Paul had a fever of 103 and was being tested for an infection. He was rude and irritable to everyone.

We were so thankful that people from Maureen's home

group were bringing us meals during this trying time. That night, we were brought a delicious pot roast. We also enjoyed an evening with friends.

Paul was totally different than the day before. He was sitting up and watched a little TV later in the afternoon. He did not go under the covers and was not irritable. The CNA did a cap shampoo on him and he shaved while she was there. He was talking about going to Maureen's and asked if Darius had a football game.

They took over a liter of fluid from his stomach. It was clear as well as his urine and blood tests were clear. His temperature went from 102 to 98 before we left. He also ate a fair amount of food.

I prayed that the Lord would imprint His Word upon Paul's mind (even upon his innermost thoughts and understanding) and that He would engrave them upon his heart (effecting his regeneration).

Paul will know You by experience and have knowledge of You. You will be merciful and gracious toward his wickedness and will remember his sins no more!

Paul was again sitting up all day. He was rude and irritable for a bit to Tory the sitter. Then he was sociable to her. The infectious disease doctor came in to say that they would know the next day if the fluid that was removed from his stomach was clear. A different psychiatrist came in and said that Paul tested fine and that the

Baker Act should be dropped. That raised a red flag with me because it was suggested by the doctor who told Paul in the beginning that he would never walk again!!! Paul was determined that he would and he did and was quite angry at that doctor.

He was still antagonistic toward me and God. Paul was fine with Maureen's visit. He cried when she played a song for him – God's Not Done With You by Tauren Wells. He really liked it, and kept saying, "that's me... this is just like me!" He choked up and could not finish listening to it. He had a beautiful heart☐

The hospital released Paul the next day because the test was clear. Coastal refused to take him back because he was not ambulatory even though he was in a wheelchair when we took him there and when they said that they would accept him after being cleared medically. We got home around 4:30, had a nice supper and evening and Maureen came over for the evening.

I thanked God for divine strength and for His promise that at the proper time we would reap if we did not give in. Galatians 6:9

The next day was very pleasant. Paul went with us to Publix, and after lunch we rode by Maureen's house, the gun range, and Ramblers Rest. The family came over in the evening to our clubhouse to celebrate three birthdays – Sammy, Maureen, and Caleb. Randy made a great boiled dinner and yum yum pudding. We went in the pool and thanked Jesus for a nice evening.

The next day, Paul was irritable off and on all day, – double-minded. He started cooking chicken wings on the oven drip pan at 550 degrees. It started smoking, and he ended up shutting it off and forgetting about them. I nicely told him that we had cookie sheets for that, but he got upset even though I was being nice about it.

Then he took a shower and fell in the shower. Ray opened the locked door to check on him, and he got VERY angry. He then took a lot of food in his room. It was beginning to look like the night of his hallucination. When I told him about the food, he again became VERY angry and told me to get out of the room. We could not reason with him so I called Maureen and thought that he would listen to her. He got ANGRY and left. We thought that he was just going out to the pool, but when he did not return, we were concerned and Ray called the police. They could not find him anywhere around.

We prayed that God would give us wisdom to know what to do and to let us speak truth to him.

God brought peace by reminding us of His Word in Romans 8:28 that he would cause all things to work together for good because we love Him. Help us, O God of our salvation for the glory of Your Name!

Office Terry stopped in to tell us that they were called to Publix where Paul was found sleeping in the bathroom.

Of course, he said that he was not. He was banned from Publix for a year. She said that he looked a mess. The last time that she saw him he was walking toward Venice Hospital.

He said that his toe was broken, but the hospital did not keep him. He was sleeping on a bench outside the hospital. Office Terry suggested a couple of programs for him. She called Viper and a program in Englewood. Paul said that he did not want to be tied to a program. I am so thankful for the way she was so caring toward him.

Ray saw Paul later in the day as he was going to Dollar General. He had a backpack and said he was gathering some gear.

As I was making some oatmeal, I heard Holy Spirit say to me, "I've seen what you have done and I will return your children from the hand of the enemy." Jeremiah 31:16-17. I saw him later in front of Goodwill and reminded him about his doctor's appointment on Monday and for him to stop by so that we could take him.

Paul showed up at our door the next morning only wrapped in a jacket and was a mess. He said that he wanted help so we let him take a shower, and we took him to the Venice ER. He was very belligerent to me and told me that he was not drinking although he told Ray that he was.

The ER doctor talked to Paul and then to us. Paul told the doctor that I was a Christian like it was a bad thing. However, the doctor said that there was nothing wrong with that. We filled the doctor in about what was going on.

He said that he would check his blood, etc. and Baker Act him! When we got home, we found a can of beer with 8.1 alcohol content.

Psalm 80 mentions restore, revive, and return several times. Father, look down on Paul and rear him and strengthen him for Yourself.

I have absolute trust and confidence in Your power, wisdom, and goodness because You are eternally changeless, always the same yesterday, and today, and forever.

Thank You for being the God of peace through Your blood Who will equip us with every good thing to carry out Your will and strengthen us to accomplish that which is pleasing in Your sight. For with God nothing is or every shall be impossible.

I was reminded of the day that I spend in worship and prayer for Paul and Holy Spirit gave me the words "warp and woof" which I discovered are terms used in weaving. Holy Spirit assured me that He would weave things together in Paul's life for good. I decreed that Paul would serve Him in holiness without fear.

Maureen went to the Venice ER to visit Paul, and they said that he was released. I called the doctor who admitted him.

 The nurse in ER checked with the nurse who attended him and said that he was still there waiting to be Baker Acted. They were looking at why they did not keep him the day before. Maureen had a good visit. He was concerned that he would not see her kids again. He had really come to love her kids. The real Paul had a beautiful heart. Paul gave Maureen a big hug when she was leaving.

God's word says that the God of peace (not fear) will soon crush Satan under your feet!!! Romans 16:20 I was determined to trust God and remain in His peace. Venice ER did not call me so I had to call them and find out that they had moved Paul to Punta Gorda . They gave me the name of the facility, but when I called that one, they said that Paul was not there and they transferred me to Riverview which was across the street from there. He was not there, but the man who answered gave me the name of Charlotte Behavioral Healthcare.

The young woman who answered said, "I can neither confirm or deny that he's here but you do not have to look any further." That young woman has the heart of a mother, and I surely hope and pray that her life has been blessed by Him! I gave her my phone number in case he wanted to contact us.

The next day, I heard, "Sunday's coming"!!! I did not know what it meant at that time.

I had been reading in Jeremiah, I was prompted to look

up the word "live" 7931 Hebrew says (cause to) remain, rest. It reminded me of Jeremiah 33:12......pastures for shepherds who rest their flocks. That word rest is 7257 rabats meaning lie (down) make to rest.

It is interesting that a couple of days before that, I saw for the first time a rabbit running in front of me on the trail near the golf course. I was thinking of "a scared rabbit"! Now here is this word that is like rabbit = rabat that means to make to rest. Thank you, Father, that You will do that for Paul.

There was a time shortly before I ended up ministering deliverance to an individual that this person told me later that he heard voices telling him, "Do not tell him that she is here"!!! So, I am convinced that all those times Paul wanted us to visit him but the demons did not!!! One time, when he was in the ER, he told the doctor that I was a Christian – was that him speaking? The doctor let him know that it was not a bad thing.

Maureen and I visited Paul in Punta Gorda that Sunday. He kept asking Maureen to get him out of there, and he was angry at me (or the demons were). The next day, Charlotte Behavioral moved him to Salvation Army Homeless in Sarasota. Thank You, Jesus. The woman at Charlotte told Maureen that they left him at Salvation Army, but he did not have to stay, and he did not. Again, there was a kind woman at the desk there that let me know that Paul did not stay even though she was not supposed to say. I prayed that God would give him beauty for ashes according to Isaiah 61:3. Father, save the son of Your maidservant. Show me a sign for good, that those who hate me may see it and be ashamed, because You, Lord, have helped me and comforted me. Psalm 86:16-17

A friend texted us and was concerned that we would not take Paul back into our home unless he was on medication and offered to help in any way. Prayer for his deliverance was what I wanted.

It was again time to search for Paul. I rode through Goodwill lot, Publix lot, and the train station. There was no sign of Paul. While I was in Sarasota earlier in the week, I rode around the streets that were close to Salvation Army. I prayed that Paul would have the mind of Christ from I Corinthians 2:16, that he would be transformed by the renewing of his mind according to Romans 12:2, and that he would come to his senses and escape from the trap of the devil having been held captive by him to do his will from II Timothy 2:26.

Thank you, Father, that Paul will be sitting at Jesus feet, clothed, and in his right mind (mentally healthy...!!!)

Went looking again for Paul at Starbucks in Venice and Sarasota. I then went to Sarasota Memorial and their ER, but he was not there. I rode up and down more streets in Sarasota. What now Lord? "Pray and wait on me"! One day I heard Holy Spirit say, "you are not doing this just for Paul because he is your son, you are doing it for Me" – loved that!

Was feeling one day like I "failed" Paul. I knew it was a lie of the enemy, but my emotions gave in to it. God is so good – he had a mutual friend of ours and Paul's send me an encouraging text that morning.

That Sunday afternoon, we had a nice afternoon at the pool with Maureen and her family. A man called Maureen from Sarasota saying he found Paul's wallet at West Coast Church in the parking lot. Ray and I met him and his wife at Marina Jack's, and he returned Paul's wallet to us – what a kind act from a stranger.

We rode all around the area near that church and some streets around Starbucks as well as going into Starbucks. We spoke to a police officer there. He thought that he possibly had seen Paul that Friday night. He took a picture of Paul's ID and was sending it to other officers.

On Monday, Maureen and I spent 4 hours driving, walking, talking to people but no leads concerning Paul. We went to Resurrection House, Starbucks, Whole Food, a thrift store, Selby Library, West Coast Church, and many parks including the one near Marina Jack's.

A lot of people were praying for Paul but still no word from him. "Be still and know that I am God; I will be exalted among the nations, I will be exalted in the earth"!

Another day, I got up at 6:00 AM so that I was able to leave home a little after 8:00 AM to look for Paul before going to Sarasota House of Prayer (S.H.O.P). I went to a 7-11 store, Resurrection House, Sarasota County Jail, walked around Gillespie Park, Selby Library, and Five Point Park.

I went to Sarasota House of Prayer from 10:15 AM until 12:00 PM. Then I decided to just quickly check out a few more places. Walked Gillespie Park again. I was halfway around Selby Library ready to head for Five Point Park. I headed across the crosswalk between Starbucks and Selby Library and could see Paul lying on the grass in the park. Thank You, Jesus!

We had a real good visit. I was able to clarify some things with him. Of course, he was glad to have his wallet and ID back. I think he liked what I wrote on a little card and put it in his wallet. It said that he had great value and was precious and loved from Isaiah 45:3. Always with a sense of humor, Paul said, "I do not even know Isaiah." I had been thinking that we should wait to hear from Paul but was reminded of Luke 15:4 that He goes after or searches until he finds the lost sheep!

He had been staying at the little field behind West Coast and said that he goes go to the 7-11 store for beer and that he liked it and was not ready to quit. Remnant Church picks up several homeless a few times a week from the park to give them lunch. He had a New Testament from them and was reading it. While we were in the park, he said, "I guess you do like me"!!! Obviously, he listens to the lies of the enemy who tells him differently. I responded by saying, "No, Paul, we drove over 5,000 miles because we do not like you and even now have spent days looking for you"!!!

I had Paul call Christina, a nice person with SSI, who was trying to get him SSI. He kept getting her answering machine so he left her a message to give permission for her to be able to ask me questions.

My prayer was, Father, I pray that You will reveal Jesus to Him and that Jesus would draw him to the Father's love." As I was asking the best way or what to pray next, Holy Spirit brought Daniel 9 and 10 to me. *Father, I will continue to pray and trust You and Your Holy Spirit to lead me and know that it is a battle between two kingdoms, but YOU WIN, JESUS!*

This all happened while I humbled my heart at Sarasota House of Prayer and received the words of Daniel 10:12, "Do not be afraid, Daniel, for from the first day that you set your heart on understanding this and on humbling yourself before your God, your words were heard, and I have come in response to your words."

The next day, I got a call from Christina of SSI who had been out on a family emergency as her 27-year-old daughter was in a similar situation so she was very understanding of Paul's situation. I told her that I would be praying for them.

A couple of days later, I spent the day at Selby Gardens in Sarasota. Paul told me previously that he wanted to go to our grandson's football game so I tried to find him around Sarasota but could not so I continued to the game in Venice.

Paul called me that night from Sarasota ER and told me that they would not keep him. He wanted us to come get him. I told him to ask for detox. He said that he would, and I told him that we would see him the next day.

I called the ER, but he was not there. I called First Step, and he was there. Thank You, Jesus. I pray that he will decide on a long-term program or have a radical encounter with Jesus. That Sunday, we visited West Coast Church with a couple of family members. We were able again to thank the man who found Paul's wallet. A few of the people there were amazed by the story.

His brother and his wife were very concerned about him. They were calling every week to see how Paul was doing. They finally said that he needed the Lord which, of course, we knew and were praying for. Later in the day, we shared our story with a couple in the pool and brought Jesus into the story. They seemed to think that "goodness" leads to eternal life. I prayed that the Father would send someone to water the seed of the Word that we had planted.

A few days later, I had lunch on Anna Maria Island at The Sandbar with my daughter. We then stopped to tour Manatee Historical Buildings. While we were there, Paul called and said that he was at Sarasota Memorial. He had to have fluid removed from his stomach and had some fluid in his lungs. He was very peaceful and said that he loved First Step.

The next day when I visited Paul in the afternoon at SMH, they had taken fluid from his lung area. He was very groggy and could not remember what we told him the day before except the score of our grandson's football game.

We did not hear from Paul for a few weeks. Then while we had some of the grandchildren staying with us, he just showed up at our home. He said that the ER released him and that First Step would not take him without hospital clearance and a Marchman Act. While he was visiting, I got to share with him that no matter what he has ever done that I will always love him.

A few days later, I talked to a woman at First Step. Usually, those people will not talk to anyone except the client, but she told me that she was going to talk to Paul about a program at Salvation Army. I prayed that he would respond positively to that.

A few days later, I called the woman at First Step. She

did not call me back. "Father, my trust is still in You to draw Paul to Yourself even if he is not interested in a program and that he will have a radical encounter with You"!

That fall I was going through all the boxes of pictures that I had to make up an album for Paul to remind him of what a happy person he used to be.

Ray and I went on a 7-day cruise for his 80th birthday. We had a great time. I continued as I had for many years to pray for Paul day and night. We arrived home at 3:00 in the afternoon and unpacked, posted some pictures, started watching the Patriots while Ray packaged items to mail. I was hungry but patient knowing he wanted to get that done. It turned out to be God's timing.

As we headed to Bogey's for something to eat, Ray saw Paul sitting at the bus stop. I did not see him and was wondering why Ray made a U-turn at the hospital. We asked him if he wanted to go with us.

We went and his niece was working, gave him a big hug, and was our waitress. We finished watching the game at Bogey's. The Patriots won. Thank you, Lord, for a wonderful way to end our fabulous week. As we were getting close to home from Miami, I wondered when we would hear from Paul again, and he was already in Venice. Great are You, Lord!!

While at Bogey's, I thought people were probably wondering what we were doing with a homeless person. My thought was, "he's my son"! Holy Spirit said, "he's mine, too"!

Paul had been staying in Sarasota so we drove him back there and told him to be sure to come and have Thanksgiving with the family. The buses do not operate on Thanksgiving and Christmas so we assured him that we would pick him up if he would call and let us know where to get him. We got to share a lot of encouraging words with Paul. He said that he belonged to Jesus and had been reading Ephesians.

I continued to come across scriptures and songs that I wanted to share with Paul the next time we saw him. Holy Spirit continued to encourage me with scripture like, "no one will ever snatch them out of My hand," "but now be courageous...for I am with you."

A couple of days later, I finished going through all my pictures for ones of Paul to make an album for him. I prayed that Paul "would tremble at His Word"! I continued to be encouraged by His Word and His Presence – "...in His Presence is fullness of joy."

About once a week, I would go to Sarasota House of Prayer (S.H.O.P) which I did a few days after we were with Paul. I was reminded once again that worship is warfare! *Draw me to it regularly, Lord.*

As I was worshipping, I heard: U-TURN. "Father, I pray that Paul would do a U-turn in his life and run to You just like Ray made that U-turn when he saw Paul at the bus stop. We had a wonderful Thanksgiving dinner with several family members but were very disappointed that Paul did not call us to pick him up.

A couple of weeks went by without hearing from him. One morning when I was on my way to S.H.O.P., I looked for Paul where we had dropped him off. He was not there so I assumed he must leave early in the morning.

I continued to be encouraged by His Presence and Word as we were not hearing from Paul. About a week before Christmas, Ray and I took a ride to Sarasota towards evening and were sitting for about an hour and a half at a couple of places where we thought Paul might show up. I was sure the Lord wanted us to go. I sensed the Spirit say, "obedience is rewarded"! We did not see Paul that night. Father, You said that our labor for You is never in vain.

We had a wonderful Christmas Eve and Christmas Day with family but still no word from Paul.

One of our readings Christmas morning was from Luke 2 when Jesus was 12, and He went to Jerusalem with His parents. On the way home, they discovered that Jesus was not with them. They went back to find Him in the temple.

After we found Paul in August in San Clemente, Paul shared that story with me. I am not sure why, but it was very encouraging to me then and on Christmas Day.

I spent a lot of time the next day making phone calls to places where Paul might have been but to no avail. It was a frustrating day, but I continued to "...cast my cares upon Him" and had a peaceful evening!

A few days later, Holy Spirit brought Jeremiah 31:16 to my mind. "Thus says the Lord: Restrain your voice from weeping and your eyes from tears, for your work shall be rewarded, says the Lord; and (your children) shall return from the enemy's land." Such a powerful promise, and it encourages me to know that "...He is watching over His word to perform it.

After Christmas, we flew to Boston for several days to celebrate my Mom's 100th birthday. It was a nice break to see my Mom, other family members, and experience a little of Boston and not be focused on finding Paul.

After we arrived home, Holy Spirit spoke these words to me, "Just as I led you to Paul, I will lead Paul to Me."

I watched a lot of the Jesus Image Conference from Orlando which proved to be a very encouraging thing for me to do as I prayed and worshipped until Holy Spirit gave further instruction and direction to find Paul. I had taken a break from continually searching around Sarasota.

A couple of weeks later, I was at S.H.O.P. in worship and prayer and kept having a vision of Bahia Vista and Beneva in Sarasota and sensed that I should go that way on the way home to look for Paul. He told me previously that he would take the bus up there to Pinecraft occasionally. I went through the parking lot of Der Dutchman and the strip mall down the street. There was no sign of Paul, and I wondered why I had that vision. I started heading home on Beneva, and there was Paul a short way down on the left at a bus stop. Thank you, Jesus! It had been 2 months since we had seen him.

He got in the van, and I pulled into the strip mall for a few minutes. I asked him if he went there because it reminded him of being raised in Pennsylvania where there were many Amish and Mennonites. He said that he thought it was. I gave him the Pizza Hut gift card from his brother, Gary and wife, Terry. Paul said, "I didn't even think that Gary liked me"! Gary never told us about Paul's parties.

 More lies! I asked him when he wanted to go there and come to our house to open his Christmas presents. He said that right away would be nice.

We went to Pizza Hut in Venice, and he ordered himself a pizza. I took a picture of him and texted it to Ray and Maureen to let them know that I had found him. We were all thrilled!

He opened all his Christmas presents. Then I gave him the picture album that I was led to make up for him of all the pictures that I had of him. He enjoyed looking at it and cried. He said that he could not believe that he was smiling in just about every picture. I said it was because he was surrounded by people who loved him and still is surrounded by people who love him. Sadly, too many people focus on a few negative events, and the enemy uses lies to convince people that their life was so negative instead of being able to remember all the love and good times.

Maureen came over to visit with us and went with us when we gave him a ride back to Sarasota. Maureen was riding in the back of the van with him and lovingly remembers Paul telling her that he needed a half a hug. She was so blessed by that.

I had gotten him a pair of Merrell hikers for Christmas at Peltz in Sarasota but returned them when we could not find him in the time frame of being able to return something.

We stopped at Peltz on the way back to Sarasota, and he picked out the pair of Merrell hikers that he wanted. He was very pleased and thankful for everything especially the Merrell hikers. He had a pair that he got in San Clemente but someone stole them when he was at Salvation Army.

They were quite expensive, and he kept saying, "I can't believe some crazy woman spent all that money for these shoes." I began to pray that every time he put them on that he would remember how much he was loved by us and God. However, I think that most of the time he kept them on so that no one would steal them.

We let Paul know that he was always welcome to come

visit us and have a meal with us. A few days later, Ray, Maureen, and I were eating lunch. Paul showed up. He had lunch with us. Then I told him that Maureen and I had already planned to go to Decision America with Jeremy Camp and Franklin Graham in Ft. Myers. Paul said, "I like road trips" to which I replied, "you would not be able to bring that backpack into the meeting." He was okay with that and rode along with us.

Oh, me of little faith, I thought that he would just sit out in the van while we attended the meeting but praise be to God, he went in with us. Paul loved the worship time with Jeremy Camp.

Franklin Graham brought a beautiful, compelling message of salvation. He did not pull any punches but named and called certain things sin yet delivered it by letting people know how much Jesus loved them. Paul stood up for salvation, and one of the staff came over to pray with him and give him a Bible. Paul had accepted Jesus as his Saviour on Christmas Eve when he was 8. As a teenager, he was baptized in water and received the Baptism of the Holy Spirit, however, after he was 18, he stopped going to church and went in another direction. God was faithful to call Paul back to Himself.

While either driving to or from Ft. Myers, Maureen and I were talking about people who have had abortions and sometimes keep it to themselves for many years before getting forgiveness and healing. Overhearing our conversation, Paul told us that he had been sexually abused by one of his father's friends when he was left with this so-called friend for the day.

It is not only sad that he was sexually abused, but he carried that around all those years. I am sure that it was one of the causes of his low opinion of himself.

A couple of days later, Paul called and said that he had stopped by but we were not home. He did stop by again, and we took him to visit his sister and family.

His aunt and uncle were there. We took him to eat at Der Dutchman on the way back to Sarasota and dropped him off at a church on Fruitville.

Ray had given him a beautiful black and red jacket that he loved. He was being loved on by everyone. However, the enemy would harass me with things like, "I could have or should have said more to him."

Again, Paul came for a visit. I was journaling, "Lord, you know that Paul is here now having arrived earlier this morning. I am trusting You regarding Words of Yours that I have written down and have been praying. I am trusting You to anoint me and give me Your words to speak that will break every yoke. You have anointed me to preach deliverance to the captives and You have chosen me and anointed me to bring forth fruit so that whatever I ask in Your Name, You will do.

Paul allowed me to lay hands on him and pray. *Father, I thank You that Your Words will not return void!!!*

Paul showed up the following Sunday at 8:30, took a shower, and went to church with us. The people gave him a great welcome and a few men prayed over him.

He spent the rest of the day with us. I took his sleeping bag and some other things to the laundromat. I also sewed his backpack.

He went with us in the evening to his sister's to watch the Super Bowl. His aunt and uncle gave him a ride back to Sarasota.

We were happy that Paul was visiting us more. A couple of days later, he came for supper and was in a real good mood. We gave him a ride back to Sarasota. I prayed, "Father, may he choose You"! I continued to pray that I would clearly hear His voice and obey as Philip did in Acts 8. Paul continued to come and visit and have meals with us.

The next Sunday, he showed up at 8:00, took a shower, and went to church with us. The Pastor and two other men prayed intense, compassionate prayers over him. They had a newcomers luncheon after the service. We all went and Paul shared where he had been and where he is now. He was touched by the love of the people. Thank You, Father, for leading us there and letting him experience that love.

Later in the day, Maureen, Caleb, and Asiah came over and gave him his belated Christmas gift. The next evening, he came at about 7:30. He was so drunk and belligerent that he could not stay! Trusting You, Father.

Several years earlier, I was reading Matthew 4 about

the people who sat in darkness saw a great light. Then He gave me the song, Morning Has Broken for Paul. It was very encouraging to know and believe that he would eventually see His great light.

He came the next day at 8:00 AM. My friend came in the afternoon for a time of prayer, and Paul joined us. In the evening, he went with us to the church we were attending at the time for Healing Prayer. Before the altar call was even given, Paul went up and laid on the floor. Two men ministered to him. One of them gave Paul his number and told him to call him when he was sober. This man had been homeless in Pittsburgh in the '80's so he had a heart to reach others in similar circumstances.

Paul came the next morning for breakfast, a shower, and a rest. We had plans for the afternoon so he left. When we got home, he was waiting outside. He told us that he called the man from church who then picked him up and took him to McDonalds to talk. His attitude was a lot better than it had been. Thank You, Lord, for him taking steps toward You.

My sister and her husband had invited Ray and I to go on a lunch cruise around Sarasota Harbor from Marina Jack's. Paul was with us so Ray suggested that we drop him off at the Remnant Church for the afternoon. We picked him up after lunch and brought him to his aunt and uncle's with us. We all played dominoes and had pizza. I think Paul really enjoyed it.

He came early the next day and spent most of the day. He was very testy off and on. Before he left, he attempted to smoke pot on our lanai and have a cigarette. He was not very happy when we said, "NO." Then he thanked us again for everything so I told him that being thankful should include respect for us and our home. Father, show us clearly what to say – how to respond!

Paul went to church again with us the next Sunday. We went to his sister's that evening to watch the movie, Harriet Tubman. Everyone enjoyed it, and we were very impressed with the courage she had and how she heard from God and obeyed. Paul watched it with us.

I walked through a room at church and saw a picture "...Be still and know...!" I saw that same scripture in the Word the day before so I was encouraged once again by God's Word.

As I read the Old Testament, I kept seeing "ashes"! It reminded me of the dream I had on August 15, 2018 where the person in the hospital swept up the "ashes". Isaiah 61:3 that says that He gives us beauty for ashes. Father, do not let me shrink back from declaring Your whole plan and purpose for him but let me know when!

Paul spent a good part of the next day with us and was very belligerent and disrespectful? We spoke to him about it before he left. I sent his friend an email. Even before that, I had an encouraging text from his friend reminding us to regularly be casting off the spirit of shame and condemnation from his life and anointing him for healing!

He came and took a shower the next day. We had several things going on that day so he left. Later, he called in a good mood and wanted to stop in. He was exhausted and in a bad mood – belligerent and disrespectful. We confronted him about it and he left. I told him that he was making his choices, but he was not going to make ours.

I thought of Philippians 1:28, "And do not (for a moment) be frightened or intimidated in anything by your opponents and adversaries (not Paul but the enemy) for such (constancy and fearlessness) will be a clear sign (proof and seal) them of (their impending) destruction but a sure token and evidence) of your deliverance and salvation, and that from God"

The next day, Paul came and was a real mess but his attitude was better. My friend was not able to make it for worship and prayer so I did it by myself. During worship, I sensed the Spirit say, "speak the words I give you"!!!

He took a shower, kept drinking, ate very little, wanted to go to his sister's. He slept most of the time that we were there. He was so drunk when we got home that he kept falling in the driveway. We watched and prayed that he would make it across the street and that he would be desperate for You!

The next day, he came around 12:30 PM, went right to the lanai and slept. Around 4:00 PM, he asked for some clean clothes. We told him that we were done making beer runs and told him how drunk he was the night before. He still denied it. We suggested that he go to the hospital.

After a while, he agreed to it. We took him to Sarasota Memorial around 5:30-6:00 pm. They admitted him and said that his platelets were low and were going to give him platelets. We left at 11:10 PM.

I prayed that he would be completely detoxed and have a sound mind and make the decision and have the desire to go to Teen Challenge or another program.

I continued to pray for complete restoration for Paul. For myself, I prayed that I would not shrink back from declaring His whole purpose and plan and to let me know when.

Father, I pray that Paul will be like a green olive tree in the house of God. I pray that he would worship and serve You! I pray that he will strive to have a clear conscience before You and men. I pray that he would walk in righteousness, self-control, honorable behavior, and personal integrity.

By faith, I apply the blood and the oil to Paul's lobe of his right ear, to the thumb of his right hand, and on the big toe of his right foot so that everything that he listens to will be holy, his hand will be an extension of the power of God, and his feet will make straight paths and go in the right direction!!!

Father, You know what is going on with Paul and what must happen. I pray that You will direct his steps to the plan that You have. We think it is Teen Challenge. What do You say? If he would be willing and obedient and submit to authority in his life, he could be set free in other ways!!!

We went to visit Paul in the afternoon. He was in a better frame of mind. Father, give us clear direction about what to say and do.

I read *Slaying Dragons* by Daniel Kolenda and read a message by James Goll on casting out demons. We know that is what Paul needs. Show us what to say or do about it.

We went to the hospital in the afternoon of the next day, and Paul was very agitated. He was trying to get out of bed and wanting his clothes. I spoke to the social worker for a while. When we went back to Paul's room, the nurses were trying to calm him down. His heart rate had spiked. She thought it was best if we left so that he would not think that we were taking him home.

She called me later and said that they were putting him in CCU until his heart rate came down and that were better equipped there to take care of him.

We visited Paul the next day in the CCU. His vitals were

good, but his ammonia was high. They had big gloves on his hands. He would get very agitated if anyone touched him. I prayed the Word of God over him quietly but out loud.

We visited Paul from 4:00 to 5:00 the next day. He was not on Presedex because his blood pressure went down. He was more aware than the day before and not quite as agitated. He still wanted to get out of there. He was still concerned about his stuff. He said that his Merrell shoes were his best Christmas present ever. I am so glad that we got those for him, and I prayed that every time he put them on that he would know how much he was loved. I would not be surprised if he slept with them on because of having a thrift shop pair of Merrell shoes stolen from him. He needed some sturdy shoes like that to help with walking.

The next day, Paul was more coherent but was still trying to get out of bed. The psychiatrist talked to us about making his decisions and will plan what comes next. Maureen said that they had to give him more meds the night before to calm him down. He was still having a lot of tremors and withdrawal going on.

When we visited Paul from 2:00 to 4:00 the next day, they transferred him to the third floor while we were there. They were weaning back the medication, he was not tied to the bed or agitated. He ate regular food all day. Thank You, Lord, for keeping him there long enough to detox and to make good decisions, hopefully!

I went to Sarasota House of Prayer in the morning and visited Paul in the afternoon. He had pneumonia, but he was more alert and in a good mood. They reduced the Adavan. As we visited, he was spacing out. I was led to ask him what he was thinking about. He said, "Dad died of pneumonia, but he had HIV and his immune system was down. I think I will be alright"! Paul said that he would not quit drinking because he did not care if he died but clearly, he does. Father, I pray that Paul will choose life.

What really blessed and encouraged me about that conversation was that I knew that Paul had forgiven his Dad. Whenever he would mention him, he would just refer to "the guy who died." If I mentioned him, Paul would say, "he's dead."

We had another good visit with Paul. He was in a good mood the whole time and asked a lot of questions about us and our family, etc. He mentioned that the hospital was not a bad place after all.

Paul spent 21 or 22 days in the hospital that time. During that time, a wonderful Christian man from Englewood drove every other day from Englewood to Sarasota to visit and pray for Paul and just be a friend for him.

When we visited Paul the next day, we had a good visit and good conversations. His friend from Englewood also visited him in the afternoon and prayed with him.

The next day, his pneumonia was cleared up, but he had a urinary tract infection. The Nurse Practitioner tried to encourage him to go to a program and not use crutches outside. He thought he could and did not want a program. Maureen came in and we talked about Celebrate Recovery. He did seem interested in that. I offered to take him to a meeting on Sunday in Venice or Thursday in Englewood.

Paul mentioned that the man who visited with him talked too much about "Religion." I continued by sharing Psalm 78 with him and why I wrote my book. I also shared that recovery centers were not places of being stuck in a room but has trees, etc. I had printed out pictures for him. I shared with him that I had people mentor me. He listened and stayed calm.

He stayed calm for about 5 days. Father, continue Your good work in Paul. Give him a hunger and a desire for Your Presence. I told him that Hebrews 4:16 says that he can come boldly to the throne of grace to obtain mercy for his failures and find grace to help in his time of need.

I let him know that "dry bones" means shame, confusion, and disappointment and that God would heal him of all of that and that the word hear in the Bible usually means obey and that God blesses us when we obey Him.

The next evening when we visited Paul, we showed him pictures of Teen Challenge near Ft. Myers and Dunklin near Okeechobee which had acres and acres of land. He could choose a job that would be outside. Paul loved being outside and working with his hands. He wanted to know how many people were there and what the sleeping arrangements were. Sarasota Memorial was trying to get him into a rehab for physical therapy.

I had a dream or vision of the physical therapy belt around Paul and God saying to me, "I've got him"! Those words were so encouraging to me.

Ray and I were going to the Van Wezel in Sarasota to see Celtic Women. We visited Paul before we went and gave him more information on Dunklin. Paul was still in good spirits yet administration was saying that he could not make his own decisions which were delaying the approval of the nursing home for physical therapy. They wanted us to sign a Power of Attorney which could cost $500???

Father, thank You for having Paul where You want him. Paul looked good and was seriously considering Dunklin. He wanted more information.

The friend from Englewood was going to have his son-in-law who lived in North Carolina call Paul because he had been there for rehabilitation.I let Paul know that there were 200 acres at Dunklin and that he could work outside making wooden shipping pallets. He framed houses in Oregon for 7 years and enjoyed that.

The next couple of days, he was very itchy and irritable. He "did not want to read John," "was not going to Dunklin to know Jesus but only because he was homeless." There seems to be a tug of war for his soul – *Jesus, You win. Paul belongs to You – what You have done, none can undo and what Your hands hold, none can snatch away!!!*

Even the psychiatrist called that Friday to say that Paul was not confused any longer and asked us what we thought. I told him about praying scriptures over his mind and his friend from Englewood praying for him every couple of days.

After church the next day, we visited Paul in the afternoon. He was up and down whether he would go to physical therapy rehab and Dunklin. At the end of the day, he seemed to be deciding on both. *Father, keep him stable. Give Him a hunger for Your Word.*

I was on my bike ride and walk around Maxine Barrett Park. Paul called me and wanted his sleeping bag and backpack. He called someone at Dunklin and had an attitude and decided not to go. I told him our conditions if he decided to be homeless. We wanted him to visit us and family and have some meals with us, but we were not going to be a homeless shelter.

When we went to visit him in the afternoon, there was a big traffic jam so we went in the evening. He never mentioned our earlier conversation. He mentioned that he might be released that Friday but never said another word about it. He was still very itchy – not sure if that was part of his irritability. He was a little sociable but sometimes not.

Let no foul or polluting language nor evil word nor un-

wholesome or worthless talk (ever) come out of your mouth, but only such (speech) as is good and beneficial to the spiritual progress of others, as is fitting to the need and the occasion, that it may be a blessing and give grace (God's favor) to those who heard it. (Ephesians 4:29)

As I was writing the above scripture, I was thinking that Paul probably knew that he messed up by getting upset with Kevin at Dunklin. It also reminded me of what I have seen in the past with some men who have failed in some way. They sometimes fall into a pit of guilt and condemnation that displays itself in pride and arrogance. *Father, set him free of guilt, condemnation, and shame and give Paul a revelation of Your love.*

Father, I thank You that "the enemy shall not exact from him or do him violence or outwit him, nor shall the wicked afflict and humble him." (Psalm 89:22)

As I read Numbers 21:4, "...and the people became impatient (discouraged) because (of the challenges) of the journey." It reminded me of what a friend said after we found Paul. "Finding Paul was the easy part"! Certainly, the challenges of the journey has been more difficult.

As I was reading Numbers 22 regarding Balaam, I thought of all the plans that fell apart regarding Paul. The woman who I met at First Step never called me back.

Salvation Army was not a good experience for Paul. Someone stole his Merrell shoes. Then Paul had the argument with Kevin at Dunklin. *Lord, are You saying that You have a better plan for Paul?*

The man from Englewood called and talked about his visit with Paul. Paul kept falling asleep, and he was angry about what I told him the day before about being homeless. This man was angry on the inside, but he prayed and God gave him peace. He told Paul that he was not going to give up on him and would take him fishing, etc. Then he prayed with Paul once again.

Father, thank You so much for sending this man into Paul's life. You surely did lead us to that church "...for such a time as this." Bless that man, Lord!

We visited Paul in the afternoon. He was not real sociable at first. I asked him if he wanted us to leave, and he said that it was up to us.

After that, he started to talk to us, and his attitude was alright. He said that he could walk without a walker. The Nurse Practitioner and another nurse came in and said that PT said that he was able to leave.

They wanted to discharge him then, but we did not have his clothes with us. We asked them about a PT Rehab. They said that he did not need it. The NP said that he had "sabotaged" his opportunity to get into Dunklin.

That was the same word that I got. He was belligerent and ended up saying that I beat him with a belt a lot (lies)!

We finally met a doctor there who ran a Homeless Café at his church. He said that unfortunately, people can be capable of making their own decisions, but some will still make bad ones.

He had on several occasions tell different doctors that I use to beat him with a belt which was not true. However, he never mentioned the things that I did not handle right so when we brought his clothes in, I talked to him about those things and asked for his forgiveness. I also told Paul that I had sent a letter to Oregon when he lived there to ask his forgiveness for things that I did and for things that I should have done. Paul said that he was not blaming anyone.

We left the hospital and drove Paul back to Venice. He wanted Ray do drop him off at the Citgo to buy beer. Ray told him that he was not going to put a nail in his coffin. Paul thanked us for everything and walked over to the Citgo. After 21 days in the hospital, I was surprised that he did that.

We went to have dinner with friends who had also lost a son. She said to me, "Keep loving your son because when they are gone, they are gone," and that is what we did right up until the end.

Paul stopped by to visit us the next day and looked terrible. What a difference a day of drinking makes! He also stopped in the next morning and was clearly already drunk. I shared Isaiah 44:20, Luke 4:18, Ephesians 5:18 and much more. I told him about reading *The Cross and The Switchblade*, the Baptism of the Holy Spirit and more. He wanted scrambled eggs but had to settle for cereal because I had other plans.

His backpack was on the lanai (mistake). I thought that he was rearranging it. When I looked closer, he was pouring a can of beer into a container and spilling it all over the floor. I grabbed the backpack and threw it outside and said that it would have to be out there in the future. Paul was angry and threatened me with not seeing him for 17 more years. I told him that if he continued to drink like that, he would not be here in 17 years.

About a week later, Paul left a note, combat boots, Fanta, and water at our doorstep for his nephew. He definitely has a heart to help people. When we were driving back from California with him, he took a homeless man into the store where we had stopped to buy him something to eat.

I kept seeing the number 5 in the night which means "grace". He surely has been giving us the grace to trust Him with Paul's life. I was also clinging to a scripture that God had given me several years before for Paul that "...the God of peace will soon crush Satan under your feet"!

Paul had not been coming around so we checked to see if he had been coming and going to the place where he stayed at across the street from us, and he had been. Then I saw him at the strip mall next door, and he told me not to be "haughty" and "arrogant" which reminded me to bind those and other spirits in him and pray and sing the Blood of Jesus over him.

A few days later, I had been thinking of asking Paul why he was allowing Satan to ruin his life and let him know that he could be delivered from demons as others had been. A young pastor had recently said, "Jesus is going to visit your camp," and Paul was at the door so I told him what I was thinking about.

I realized that Paul was able to apply for the stimulus check so I went across the street to tell him that I applied for it for him. During this time, I was continuing to spend a lot of time in soaking prayer and praise and worship for Paul and others and that I would hear clearly what God wanted me to do.

A week or more later, we were at our condo pool when a neighbor on the third floor on the street side of the building said that he saw Paul on the sidewalk in the morning. He said that a cruiser came, then another cruiser came and an ambulance. I called Venice ER, and Paul was there.

They were waiting for blood tests to admit him. He was admitted late in the afternoon but did not have a room until later that night. I was finally able to talk to a nurse at 9:00 PM. She said that they were treating him for alcohol and an infection. They would not have the culture results for 72 hours. I then called his room, but he did not answer. During this time, I kept playing the song "Goodness of God" and crying and wishing that I could hold Paul in my arms, and God said to me, "I am holding him in Mine"!

Paul was negative for Covid – praise God! This was a time when Covid was everywhere and the hospitals were not allowing visitors. He called the next day and told me that he had to crawl out of his camp area (which is what I thought) because of his neuropathy as if that was all that was ailing him. He was in a lot of denial about his alcohol and did not want to read or hear anything about it.

He was in Venice Hospital for about a week. One day, a nurse called and said that Paul wanted me to bring his walker to the hospital as they were checking him out. I said that I absolutely would not bring him a walker to try to maneuver at his camp in the woods. I told her that he needed to be in a PT rehab. She ended up calling me back at some point to say that he was being transferred to a rehab in Englewood which was good news.

Paul called me to wish me a happy Mother's Day. Again, there were no visitors allowed there. I told him that the stimulus check had arrived. He was very happy at the rehab with the people and food and was not in a hurry to get out of there as he had been in previous hospital stays. I continued to pray that he would completely surrender his life to the Lord.

I talked to him a few days later. He still was not interested in any program and adamant about not needing any help! After being in Englewood for two weeks, he was released the day after we talked. We picked him up in the afternoon, took him to the bank to deposit his check.

Then we went to Walmart where he bought a phone, a tent, a sleeping bag, a light, jacket, and a watch. He came back to our house to get his phone activated.

He left shortly afterwards so we decided to go out to eat. We saw him crossing the street to head to the gas station. The next day, he wanted me to take him back to Walmart to exchange his sleeping bag. Then he wanted to go to Maxine Barrett Park to walk around. When we got there, he could see the ocean and headed right for it. He loved the ocean, but this was the first time that he got to go since he was in Florida. We spent over an hour there enjoying the sounds and sights of the ocean as well as chatting quite a bit. It was a wonderful time which I was very happy for. As we were heading back to the van, he slid on some rocks as he was going down a small hill and bruised his face and knee. I felt so bad for him.

On the way home, Paul became very argumentative and was quite upset with me. As I am writing this, I am remembering another time many years ago when I spent a week in a cottage on the beach at Hilton Head with my four children and two grandchildren. We had a wonderful time, and Paul and I spent a lot of time playing cards together. On the way home from there, he also became very agitated. I am not sure what that is all about. I am thinking that he does not like to see good times come to an end.

A couple of days later, he came to visit in the late afternoon and stayed for supper. He set up the voicemail on his phone and was in a good mood. After he passed away and his phone was still active, I loved calling his phone and hearing his voice, "this is Paul"!

A couple of days later, we had a beautiful afternoon at the beach with Maureen, her kids, and Paul. After Maureen left and before she came, he was belligerent for no reason. So again, after a wonderful time, he acts up. I do not always respond as I probably should and told him that he was part of the ungrateful, entitlement generation. He left angry and said that he would see us in 2044!

I had a text on my phone at 11:21 PM that night that Paul had been admitted to Venice Hospital for alcohol withdrawal – electrolytes. He was still in the hospital the next day which was the day before his 51st birthday. He was not around for his 50th so we wanted to have a big celebration for his 51st. I prayed that it would be possible.

So, we planned his party. Maureen and her family decorated the club house with balloons and streamers. Paul called in a good mood and attitude to see what time his party was. He came around 1:00 PM and hung out.

Then he went to the bank and store with Ray and came back later. I made one of his favorite meals – chicken alfredo which turned out good. I ordered him a cake from Publix so that there would be enough for everyone. He wanted to know where his cheesecake was so I told him that I would make one for him the next week.

Everyone gave Paul a card – some gave him gifts. He was so pleased. *Thank You, Father, for this time to celebrate his birthday for the first time in 18 years*. He went home with his nephew for the night. A couple of days later, I made the cheese cake for Paul. He came for supper of macaroni and cheese. We went in the pool while the cheese cake was in the oven and had a very peaceful day. *Thank You, Lord!*

I was going to get Paul a watch for his birthday, but he already bought himself one so, I planned to take him to Marina Jack for his gift. So, a couple of days after his birthday, Paul and I went to Marina Jacks for lunch. On the way there, we stopped at a store so that he could get some batteries. He came out with some white artificial carnation flowers for me. They are not my favorite thing, but I still have them and will not part with them.

We also went to Siesta Beach and he thoroughly enjoyed being in the water and resting on the beach. I then drove him to Dick's Sporting Goods because he had a gift certificate but could not find anything he wanted. We had a wonderful day, but when I would not let him drink in the van, he got very angry and told me that I was the grouchy one. So once again, a wonderful day turns sour!

At the end of May, we went to Maureen's to celebrate his niece's birthday. Paul went with us but his behavior was not appropriate. When we left, he almost stumbled down the steps. After we got back to our condo, I believe that this was the night that we wondered if he would make it across the busy highway because he kept falling as he walked out of our driveway. We did not see much of Paul in the coming days. If we did not see him around, Ray or I or both of us would go across the street where he was camping out to check on him.

On June 18, 2020, I had a dream that Paul had died. I went across the street to see Paul and told him about my dream and asked him if he would please do something so that this dream would not come true. I also told him that the worst thing for parents was to lose a child. He just looked at me as if I was crazy. I prayed that Paul would humble himself and cry out to Jesus for deliverance!

That Sunday, the family was planning a celebration for my birthday and for Father's Day. Paul called me around 1:30 and said that he would be a little late but never showed up.

Ray and I enjoyed celebrating my birthday and our anniversary that week. On the 24th in the early evening, Ray and I went across the street to see Paul. He was not at the place that he usually camped. Ray said, "well, he's up and around," and we just thought that he would be back very shortly. We were reading in bed when there was a knock on our door shortly after 9:00 P.M. It was someone from the Sheriff's office who wanted to come in and speak to us.

He came in and said, "Paul is deceased"!!! It was a total shock. He then said that someone found Paul laying on his backpack at the bus stop in Venice between Route 41 and Jacaranda. It seems like he apparently went to sleep and never woke up. Even though Paul's liver was somewhat damaged, the coroner said that he died of natural causes. He was out in 95 degree weather for days without water. I notified some family members and just sat in shock for the next several hours.

One of the ways that God helped me through this was by sitting with my journal the next morning and thanking Him for all that I could think of. I was so thankful that He sent us to California and did find him and bring him back to Florida with us. He got to know how much his family loved him and was amazed that so many people were praying for him.

I was thankful that Paul was in Venice the last 5 months

of his life, and we could usually find him. I am so thankful that I made Paul a photo album of pictures of him. He was able to see all the beautiful pictures of himself and family and the good times that were had. It made him cry to see how loved he was and wonder what happened?

He was so thankful that we got him the Merrell hikers. He absolutely loved them and could not believe the money that was spent on them. It was money well spent. I would pray that every time that he put them on his feet, he would remember how loved he was.

I was so thankful that we got to celebrate his 51st birthday in the clubhouse with the family. I made him chicken alfredo which was one of his favorite meals that he use to request for his birthday. I got him a cake from Publix so that there would be enough for the family but made him a cheese cake that he requested the next week.

I was so thankful for the couple of times that I spent with him at the beach and Marina Jack's. I continue to be thankful that Paul went to the Franklin Graham meeting in Ft. Myers with Maureen and I. He loved it – Franklin and the music of Jeremy Camp.

He stood up and once again committed his life to Christ. He had accepted Jesus as his Savior when he was 8 and was baptized in the Holy Spirit and water when he was 13 or 14.

I was so thankful that he went to church with us a few times and publicly stood up at a luncheon and confessed his acceptance of Christ. I was so thankful for the Pastor there and all the other men who reached out to Paul and prayed with him and one of them who visited him a lot in the hospital.

At first, it was sad to look across the street and know that Paul was not there, but Jesus reminded me that He loved Paul a lot more than I did and saw his suffering and took him home to be with Him. *Thank You, Jesus!*

In My Father's house are many mansions; if it were not so, I would have told you. I go to prepare a place for you. And if I go and prepare a place for you, I will come and receive you to Myself, that where I am, there you may be also. (John 14:2-3)

Proverbs 25:25 says, "As cold water to a weary soul, so is good news from a far country." It sure was good news that Garrett contacted us in 2018 to let us know where Paul was. It was also very good news when Garrett, Ray and I found him in August of 2019 in Laguna Beach. So thankful for that and for Garrett.

When I would get up in the morning, I had what I would call a blah feeling; but as soon as I got in the Word of

God, it would lift. There was also something that I could not put my finger on; but when I went to a conference several months later, the speaker was talking about a spirit of death and mentioned several other things associated with it – one being a spirit of heaviness. As I traveled home, I knew that is what I was dealing with. I broke off a spirit of heaviness and started to praise the Lord. Isaiah 61 says that God comforts ALL who mourn and that He gives us a garment of praise for the SPIRIT of heaviness. He truly is faithful to His Word so that we do not have to be in emotional pain and grieving for the rest of our life.

I had a dream the night after his passing that we were in a church somewhere and Maureen came in with Paul, and I thought in the dream, "oh, he is still alive." Yes, he is alive with Jesus. God's Word says, "We are confident, yes, well pleased rather to be absent from the body and to be present with the Lord." (II Corinthians 5:8)

The day was quiet making calls, texts, messages and receiving calls. We went to Maureen's in the afternoon and Randy and Maureen stopped in later.

We needed to find a funeral home for cremation and talk to the Pastor about a memorial service. Ray and I met with Gulf Coast Cremation to make the arrangements with them. I then thought about writing an obituary.

I thought about one of the days on the way home from California with Paul. I asked him how I should pray for homeless people. He said, "to have courage, perseverance, and confidence"! Paul had all those attributes.

When David lost his baby son, he said in II Samuel 12:23, "I shall go to him, but he shall not return to me." Again, I was thankful that Paul believed in Jesus as His Savior and has eternal life with Him and that someday we will go to be with Paul, Jesus, and many other loved ones.

A couple of days later, I cried a lot and could feel the pain of missing Paul and realizing that I would not see him until I go to heaven. I was glad that Maureen had one of the kid's birthday party at the pool! It was very refreshing. Before the week was over, we picked up Maureen, went to Bogey's for supper and had a sleepover and looked at lots and lots of pictures. Before we brought her home the next day, we went to Peach's for breakfast. It was wonderful to have this supportive time.

I had finished the obituary and mailed it to my Mother, his brother Gary, and his wife Terry as well as emailing it to friends. Later, I was looking through the pictures that Paul sent me from New Mexico and Arizona. I found a picture of Paul rock climbing that looked just like the picture of someone rock climbing with the scripture Psalm 61:2 on it that I had prayed for Paul every night when my head hit the pillow. "…. When my heart is over-whelmed; lead me to the rock that is higher than I."

After I wrote Paul's obituary, I had it placed in the Lancaster, PA newspaper because that is where Paul grew up and had many friends there. Maureen received a phone call from one of his friends who said that several would be watching his memorial service on Zoom. He also sent some pictures of Paul and said that Paul's friend, Jeremy, would be coming from North Carolina.

Maureen and I had both prepared some things to share about Paul at the service. We had some beautiful flowers and an album as well as picture collage that Maureen made up. Many people from the church attended as well as people from Maureen's home group who we also knew, and all family who were in the area.

Paul's friend, Jeremy and his wife Julia were there from North Carolina. It was her birthday and their anniversary. Julia had never met Paul, but she knew how much Jeremy loved him and knew that they would be at the service rather than celebrating her birthday and their anniversary. That was so special.

Jeremy told us that every time that there was a wedding or other get together with all their friends in Lancaster, they would all be asking each other if anyone heard from Paul. He was very much loved and appreciated by all his friends. I prayed that Paul's life and salvation would touch many people to be saved and come to know Jesus.

I continued to journal in the days ahead. "Father, I miss Paul and really thought it would turn out different. Help me to trust You the way You want me to, to be at peace, and work with You to establish Your Kingdom on this earth while I am here."

"What if we could all see what they are doing in heaven! Would we be joyful with them? I read about heaven in Revelation."

A lot happened in the last 10 months. Paul was in and out of the hospital several times in Venice and Sarasota. People would ask me if I was tired. My response was that I was exhausted but I would rather be exhausted and know where my son was than not know. We visited him every day and Maureen and her family visited him quite often in the hospital and at our house.

Paul kept adamantly refusing to go in a program even though he was told that he would die if he did not stop drinking. He said that he did not care because he did not have a wife or children.

I even offered at one point for Ray and I to minister to him as we have ministered to a lot of other people. Like many people, I really do not think that he wanted to go to the places of hurt, past sin, etc.

On the night of June 24th, we had a knock on the door. I thought that it was Paul and that he wanted help. It was a detective from the sheriff's office telling us that Paul was deceased. Up until that moment, I believed with all my heart that Paul would eventually surrender totally for deliverance and healing prayer. I do not regret walking in that faith because it is what kept me from being stressed out about him and walking in peace.

On the 26th, I was reading Philippians 3:21, "...that He would transform and completely refashion our earthly bodies so that we would be like His glorious resurrected body. Paul now has that glorious body which he so badly needed.

As I thought about that, the Apostle Paul's words were coming to me where he said that it was his desire to leave this world and be with Christ. I paged back and found it in chapter 1 which is what we read on the 24th when Paul passed.

This is not what we prayed or believed for but I believe that it was Paul's desire to be with Jesus.

He loved Maureen and her family and loved getting to know his younger nieces and nephews and get re-acquainted with Hannah and Sammy, the older ones. They all loved him, and he loved them.

That morning, I thought of the Word in John 14 where Jesus said that in My Father's house there are many mansions......I will come back again and I will take you to Myself so that where I am you may be also.

As I looked across the street one day, I was saddened to think that Paul is not there, but right away that Word from John came to me and I was comforted to know that Paul is with Jesus never to suffer again. We do surely miss him though.

Maureen posted a video that talked about praying for your kids, teaching them to pray, teaching them about generational sin, etc. I wrote in my journal and told God that I did all that – what happened. He said, "you do not know now but someday you will" so I rest in that in the midst of missing him.

Pastor Emily gave a good Word a couple of weeks ago about "returning to the Lord." After that, I heard, "Only in returning to me and resting in me will you be saved. In quietness and confidence is your strength." God is good!

Father, I miss Paul and really thought it would be different. Help me to trust You the way You want me to, to be at peace, and work with You to establish Your Kingdom while I am here. I was so thankful for the support of family. Maureen came over one night with stuffed shells and had a sleep over. We spent the evening looking at Paul's album – such wonderful memories.

A few weeks later, I was blessed by a prophetic word from Andrew Towe. "It's Not Over! The Lord would have me prophesy to you, "It is not over! That which has been lost to you has exited your life for My divine purpose. Do not fear. I am working My plan. Trust Me. You will see My miraculous power!"

Little by little, I was regaining my strength and getting things done like recording and putting away sympathy card and pictures of Paul that were on the display boards for his memorial service.

We were thinking about taking our usual trip to Pennsylvania and New England to visit family and friends and just felt the need to get away. This was during Covid so we got tested. After we got tested, I remembered that Paul was happy that he tested negative. It seems like he was giving mixed messages about wanting to live. He did the same thing when he had pneumonia and mentioned that his father died of pneumonia. It made me sad.

I was also sad as I read an Amish story and someone's boyfriend left to go in CO service, she said, "I always felt that he was never meant to stay"! I never actually had that thought, but maybe deep down, I knew.

When we got the negative results, we headed north. We had a good trip, but when we turned onto Route 17 that goes through Virginia to Pennsylvania; I became very emotional as I thought, "we were bringing Paul home"! Paul's real home is in heaven with Jesus, but Pennsylvania is where he grew up.

The next morning, the Holy Spirit brought me comfort from the words of Habakkuk 3:17-18, "Though the fig tree may not blossom, nor fruit be on the vines; though the labor of the olive fail, and the fields yield no food; though the flock may be cut off from the fold, and there be no herd in the stalls – yet I will rejoice in the Lord, I will joy in the God of my salvation.

Visiting friends in Pennsylvania, some who knew Paul and some who did not was comforting to share his story. At one friends' home, we were so blessed after dinner by sitting in the living room around the piano, listening to their testimonies as one played the piano and another the cello. His Presence was so evident with us.

A couple of days later, we spread some of Paul's ashes at Chickies Rock County Park between Columbia and Marietta overlooking the Susquehanna River where Paul often spent time with friends jumping in the river from a rope swing. This day brought a range of emotions. One was bittersweet as we were walking up a hill carrying his ashes, I remembered that when he was quite young and we would go on a family hike, Paul would usually say, "carra" meaning that he wanted to be carried so here we were hiking in the woods carrying him once again.

After spending a couple of weeks in Pennsylvania, we traveled to Massachusetts and had a wonderful cookout and visit with several family members. We then proceeded to go to Maine.

After being there for several days, there were some things happening that were causing me some emotional pain. As I was processing it, I realized that I was tapping into the emotional pain of not seeing Paul for 17 years and wondering why. Through the years, I was concerned about him and prayed for him a lot but never allowed myself to experience the pain. Sometimes I would if for instance I saw a man with a good relationship with his mother. I wondered how could a son not contact his mother who loved him so much.

Of course, I knew from having conversations with Paul that he believed so many lies as many people do. He really thought that I did not like him yet I thought that he was amazing. I had to remember the things that he said when he was not in a double-minded state like back at the hotel in California. Paul said, "Mom, did I ever say the L word – I love you." The Lord allowed me to see that it was always a spiritual battle with Paul.

I sensed Holy Spirit say to me, "He is with Me now and KNOWS the Truth. I want you to KNOW the Truth, also. Paul loved you and his family." "So, if the Son sets you free, you are free indeed"! John 8:36

After Paul passed, we were sharing his story of finding him in California and all that transpired. Some thought that I should write a book about Paul because it surely was miraculous to find him. Some people were in tears as I shared the story of finding him. I hope and pray that people will see what an amazing talented and loving person that Paul really was. Yet, as I mentioned earlier, doctors diagnosed him as being schizophrenic which Paul knew and I am sure that it was a great source of embarrassment for him. Thus, the drinking problem and not wanting to be around the friends and family who loved him.

My father spent 22 years in Worcester State Hospital in a psychiatric ward having been diagnosed with schizophrenia. Jeremiah 32:18 says, "You show lovingkindness to thousands, and repay the iniquity of the fathers into the bosom of their children after them – the Great, the Mighty God, whose name is the Lord of hosts." The bosom is our emotional structure. Sadly, Paul had some of my father's generational sins/curses in his life.

I do not look at things the same way that the medical field does. Generational sins/curses can be broken off people in the Name of Jesus Christ. Jesus came to heal the brokenhearted and set the captives free – Luke 4:18. I so wish that Paul would have come to receive all that God had for him, but I do know that he is with Jesus and is fully healed and restored.

John 10:10 says that the thief (Satan) comes to rob, kill, and destroy but that Jesus came to give us life and give it to us abundantly. If you or anyone of your loved ones is not experiencing this abundant life, be born again – receive Jesus Christ as your Savior and Lord, be baptized in water, be baptized with the Holy Spirit, seek deliverance and inner healing, and know that God loves you and wants you to experience His abundant life.

About the Author

MARGARET ABBOTT lives in Florida with her husband, Ray. They have 7 adult children (1 in heaven, 15 grandchildren (1 in heaven), and 9 great-grandchildren. Margaret has shared her story in Maine, Pennsylvania, Florida, Nova Scotia, Costa Rica, Zambia, South Africa, Mozambique, and Mexico.

You have a story.
We want to publish it.

Everyone has as a story to tell. It might be about something you know how to do, or what has happened in your life, or it may be a thrilling, or romantic, or intriguing, or heartwarming, or suspenseful story, starring a cast of characters that have been swimming around in your imagination.

And at Wyatt & Sons Publishers, we can get your story onto the pages of a book just like the one you are holding in your hand. With professional interior design and a custom, professionally designed cover built just for you from the start, you can finally see your dream of being an author become reality. Then, you will see your book listed with retailers all over the world as people are able to buy your book from wherever they are and have it delivered to their home or their e-reader.

So what are you waiting for? This is your time.

visit us at

www.wyattpublishing.com

for details on how to get started becoming a
published author right away.

www.ingramcontent.com/pod-product-compliance
Lightning Source LLC
Chambersburg PA
CBHW040207060426
42445CB00036B/1976